Helping a Child
Understand Death

Helping a Child Understand Death

by
LINDA JANE VOGEL

FORTRESS PRESS
Philadelphia

Library of Congress Catalog Card Number 74–26325
ISBN 0–8006–1203–5

Third printing 1981

9189F81   Printed in the United States of America   1–1203

Dedicated
TO THE GLORY OF GOD
in loving memory of my father
SAMUEL PETER BAKER
and
in thanksgiving and hope for my son
PETER JONATHAN VOGEL

Contents

Preface

Perhaps it will help you to know why this book came
to be. Like most people, I never really gave much
thought to the meaning of death until it struck close
to me. But watching my father die a long and
dehumanizing death forced me to face death
squarely—and try to help my children develop a
healthy attitude toward it as well.

In large part, then, this book is autobiographical. It
is the result of my own journey to understand and
accept death and to explain it to my children. Without the encouragement, insight, help with the
housework, and love of my husband Dwight, this
book could never have been written.

In addition, I discovered in the workshops I was
leading that many church school teachers had experienced disturbing encounters with death. They
expressed the need and desire for help in exploring
its meaning.

The opportunity for uninterrupted reflection and
research came when my husband and I were accepted as Fellows of the Institute for Ecumenical
and Cultural Research at St. John's Abbey and University in Collegeville, Minnesota, where we spent

an academic year while on sabbatical leave from Westmar College in LeMars, Iowa.

I have tried to intertwine my own understanding of death with an approach for helping children explore its meaning. The book is not intended as "the answer" to the problem of death. My hope is rather that it can be a guide for helping Christians find their own answers, answers that they can live with—and die with—in the knowledge of Jesus Christ, our Lord.

ONE

Why, God, Why?

Oh Lord, how long shall I cry for help, and thou
wilt not hear?   *Habakkuk 1:2*

MY STRUGGLE TO FIND MEANING IN DEATH

When you're young and have a loving husband,
healthy children, and a meaningful job, life seems
good. Death seems remote and you rarely give it
a thought. That's the way it was for me a few years
ago.

I accepted the traditional Christian beliefs about
death without any problem at all. My grandmother
had died when I was fourteen and I cried a lot on the
way to the cemetery, but she was old and my beliefs
about death got me through the experience without a
hitch.

Then, suddenly, my world spun out of focus. It
happened on Labor Day. My father noticed a blind
spot in one eye. The explanation was that a blood
vessel had burst. At Thanksgiving he spent ten days
in the hospital with "malfunctioning kidneys."
Christmas brought a severe case of "stomach flu."
January brought a violent seizure and an unfruitful

period of extensive testing. It wasn't until March that we knew we were watching my father struggle and suffer in a losing battle against a milignant brain tumor.

At the age of fifty-nine he lost his ability to do his job. He became less and less able to do or say what he intended, but was still alert enough to recognize that fact. He would try over and over to make his wishes known, becoming more and more frustrated because we couldn't understand what he was saying.

Gradually he lost control of his bodily functions. And because the tumor caused pressure in his brain, he was sometimes unreasonable in his demands on those he loved.

Why, I asked, could God let this thing happen to my dad, who had been a good man and always put others before himself? Why, God, why?

And then I felt guilty for questioning. How could I presume to be a Christian when I had so many doubts?

I prayed. I searched. I felt guilty. But I could not accept or understand.

I had never before experienced the deep loneliness which I felt as I struggled with the knowledge that my dad was dying. What did all this mean for my life and my faith?

My husband sensed my aloneness and pain. He gave me a copy of Dag Hammarskjold's *Markings*, inscribed with these words:

> For heights of happiness
>   From depths of love
> With one who cares
>   But cannot share
>   the burden of your solitude
> But waits and prays
>   in the community of the Spirit
>   which makes us one.

Confronting death brings us face to face with ourselves. We cannot but search for the meaning of life when we try to understand death. But why must we add to our burden by feeling guilty about our questioning?

Something seemed wrong. I was certain during those months that my faith in God was real and important to me. At the same time, the loneliness, pain, and guilt, and the need to understand were equally real. I was plagued by the seeming contradiction and wondered: Am I *really* a Christian?

After two years of anguish, innumerable trips to Kansas to be with my mother and dad, the ordeal of surgery, the full sequence of cobalt treatments, and incessant but seemingly futile prayers for restored health or the blessing of death, I left with my husband and children for a much-needed three-week camping trip.

One evening after an especially enjoyable drive in the Canadian Rockies, I put pajamas on our four-year-old Peter and our two-year-old Kris, and had them stretch out in the rear of our VW camper while we headed back toward our campsite. My husband, Dwight, and our seventeen-year-old, Mark, were in the front, and after I had Peter and Kris comfortably settled I moved up to the jump seat to view the scenery.

The children were tired and quieted down at once. But the silence was broken by our then-untalkative Kris. She said, "Pete gone. Pete bye-bye."

I turned around and was horrified to discover the back door open—and no Peter!

"My God, he's gone! He's gone!" I screamed. I knew in my heart that he was dead. Dwight screeched the brakes, wheeled the camper around and began the search. We looked on the road, in the ditch—everywhere—for our son. After what seemed like forever we came around a curve to a pull-off where we found Peter safely in the arms of a Canadian woman.

I leaped from the car while Dwight was still braking, and the first thing Peter said to me was, "Mommy, you shouldn't get out of the car while it's moving. You might fall on your face."

I breathed a prayer: "Thank you, God. He's alive." And then more unspoken prayers as we drove quickly to the ranger station. We learned that it was thirty miles to the nearest doctor.

Peter was conscious and I worked to keep him awake. By the time we arrived at Pincher Creek

Hospital, he was screaming from pain and fright.

For three nights and days I sat by his bed as the doctors waited to be sure all was well. Peter would drop off to sleep and then his legs would begin moving as if he were running. "Stop, Daddy, stop!" he would cry and we would wake him up to assure him he was all right.

Whenever I dropped off to sleep in my chair I would be jolted awake by visions of that open door and no son. What if there had been a car behind us? What if he had hit the guard rail, like his stuffed pig—we had found Porkchop, split open, part way down the mountainside?

Then I would relive that instant when I first took Peter in my arms—and prayed. That was the moment I experienced most vividly God's revelation to me. I had stood apart with my son in my arms and watched that brilliant ball of fire which is the evening sun drop ever so gently behind the majestic mountain peaks. The terror of those frightful minutes when I feared Peter was dead was suddenly transformed into thanksgiving; for indeed, a son is given!

God's revelation to me in that brief moment is the most real thing I have to share from my personal struggle with the meaning of life and death: God gives life, and God takes life away, and the taking away is so terribly painful because what he gives is so very good.

For months I had been unable to accept the fact that my father was slowly dying from an incurable cancer of the brain. Now, suddenly, I knew in the depths of my being that God *is*, that he *does* love, and that I could say, "Father, into your hands I give my life, my dad, my son!"

BEING ANGRY—FEELING GUILTY—FINDING ACCEPTANCE

The struggle we face when death strikes close is real. Our first reaction is probably, "It can't be true." We can deny the truth for awhile, but then we must accept the situation for what it is.

The insurance advertisements mislead us when they say: "*If* you die, she get's plenty of help." The truth is *when* not *if*. Each of us *will* die. Death is a part of life. It is real. It is intensely personal. We cannot escape death or avoid it. It will not go away simply because we refuse to believe it is happening.

When we realize that death is for real we often get angry. Why, God, why? Why my dad? Why now? Why this way? We ask questions but we are not looking for logical answers. Our mind is not in control. Frustration, resentment, and anger will not be satisfied with rational answers.

As I look back, I am convinced that these powerful negative feelings are not bad. They are human responses to the loss and helplessness we feel when someone we love deeply is dying. I felt great relief when a friend pointed out to me that we need not worry or feel guilty about blaming God in our despair and anger. "Don't worry about God," my friend said. "He doesn't need us to defend him. He can take it. God understands!"

Sometimes we try to bargain with God: "If only you'll make dad well, God, I'll go into the ministry." These "fox-hole" promises are one way in which we try to handle death when it comes close. They are expressive of a stage many people go through on their way toward an acceptance of death.

Often we try to comfort someone by saying, "Don't cry!" But tears are one way of expressing ourselves and of releasing the grief we feel. We need to be free to cry, even as we need openly to express our anger. We are sad as we begin to experience separation from someone who has been important to us. At such a time depression is a normal stage which we go through in our struggle to find meaning in life and death.

For me, real acceptance of death came as a gift. After months of struggle and guilt and pain, I realized that it was OK. My anger was OK; my depression was OK; I was OK. God loves me! He understands! He cares for me even in my doubt and loneliness. He accepts me just as I am. And if *he* can accept me, *I* can accept me too. I can accept my father's dying. Accepting life as it is means accepting life and death.

More trips to Kansas followed, but my feelings of doubt and guilt were no longer dominant. It was still painful to see my father suffer, but now I was aware of real strength from a loving God. The first anniversary of my father's death was on an Easter Sunday—a meaningful reminder of God's grace and acceptance and love.

WHAT CAN WE SAY?

Often people try to avoid talking about death and dying. We sometimes put off making that hospital call we should make because we simply don't know what to say—we are afraid. This feeling of perplexity and uneasiness in the face of death is not unique to our age. Tolstoy expressed it powerfully in a novel he wrote in 1886:

> What tormented Ivan Ilych most was the deception, the lie, which for some reason they all accepted, that he was not dying but was simply ill, and that he only need keep quiet and undergo treatment and then something very good would result. He however knew that do what they would nothing would come of it, only still more agonizing suffering and death. This deception tortured him—their not wishing to admit what they all knew and what he knew, but wanting to lie to him concerning his terrible condition, and wishing and forcing him to participate in that lie.[1]

Somewhat later in the book Ivan thinks to himself, "This is wrong, it is not as it should be"; all man lives for "is falsehood and deception," which hides both life and death.[2]

The tendency to playact is real. But the need to face the truth and talk about dying and death is terribly important. Mrs. Vincent Lombardi, wife of the famed Green Bay Packer's football coach, said in an interview following his death: "We played little games. In the beginning, he was going to lick it. He wasn't a gabby type. He shut me out." But, she admits, she shut him out too: "He tried to talk to me once. He tried to talk about dying and I said, 'Vin, I don't want to talk about it.' I robbed him of a chance to tell me things. I'll never forgive myself. I thought there was time. . . ."[3]

The truth is that you and I and all human beings will come to an end. Death is a part of life. Coming to terms with death can free us to come to terms with life. We must begin talking about death—talking with each other and with our children.

In the not-too-distant past sex was a taboo subject. People falsely assumed that children did not have any sexual feelings and therefore sexuality was not a problem and should not be discussed. Now we run the risk of shifting our taboo from birth and the beginning of life to death and the end of life. We are tempted to rationalize once again that children cannot comprehend death and so the subject should be avoided.

Somehow we need to begin talking about death

and dying as the intrinsic part of life that it is. When we can face it in truth ourselves we will be able to begin helping our children.

Many people, at least in their subconscious, are convinced that they are immortal. Death is seen as an individual accident rather than a universal fact. We require legal forms certifying the "cause of death." We blame the disease, the accident, the physiological change that comes with old age—all in an attempt to hide from the fact that we all will die.

We usually refrain from speaking about death in the presence of the dying. If we discuss it at all we do so behind their back or outside their door— sometimes in ways that imply we're glad it's happening to them rather than to us. We refuse to face the fact that death will, in fact, come to us as well.

Children often embarrass adults by speaking bluntly about death. How would you feel if your child approached your dad and asked with compassion, "Grandpa, when are you going to die?" Embarrassed? Uncomfortable? Angry? Children can help adults face death honestly. The next time a child raises the topic of death, perhaps instead of stifling his inquiry and forcing our taboos upon him we should ask ourselves why we feel as we do.

FEAR AND THE GOOD NEWS

Sometimes fear is the thing which dominates our attitudes toward life and death. Fear of life makes us afraid to face the future and fear of death makes us afraid to give up the future. Fear can make us its slave.

To the extent that fear dominates our response to life and death, we cripple our children. God as revealed in and through Jesus Christ wants us to respond not in fear but in faith and love. Fear can never be the basis for a meaningful relationship with him.

To portray God as the all-knowing Father who punishes us when we are bad, and to depict death as that fearful day when we will be punished if we were "bad" and rewarded if we were "good" cannot lead the child to any kind of meaningful faith response. News like this is not *good* news—it is not the gospel of Jesus Christ! The good news is that "God shows his love for us in that while we were yet sinners Christ died for us" (Rom. 5:8).

All of us are sometimes weighed down by fear. But the Christian faith provides the answer. God's perfect love casts out fear. When we use our religion to perpetuate fear it is no longer the good news of our Lord and Savior, Jesus Christ.

Within this context, then, our encounters with death need to be shared with our children. When the children are included in our discussions and expressions of sorrow and grief, they will grow in their understanding of life and death. They will come to see death as an important part of life.

But we must not fall into the trap at this point of

denying death and asserting that we do not really die but live forever in heaven. Death is real. It is the end of man's pilgrimage on earth. It is the end of human life and human relationships *in our world.* Our bodies return to dust.

To talk about heaven before we face the truth that all men die is not hope but escapism! Resurrection is meaningless unless death is real. Paul's affirmation that "in Christ shall all be made alive" loses its power apart from his prior assertion that "in Adam all die" (1 Cor. 15:22).

The Christian does, in fact, meet death with hope. The language my grandmother once used to talk about dying is not language I feel comfortable using; yet I know that she met death as a friend and not an enemy. The Christian gospel is, indeed, good news—we need fear neither life nor death. We are free to face death openly with our children and to meet it with faith and hope whenever we encounter it.

TWO

Understanding a Child's Understanding

> Then children were brought to him that he might lay his hands on them and pray. The disciples rebuked the people; but Jesus said, "Let the children come to me, and do not hinder them; for to such belongs the kingdom of heaven."
>
> *Matthew 19:13–14*

DEATH AROUND US

We are not free to decide whether or not we will shield our children from confrontation with death. Children today encounter death as an everyday occurrence. The news is full of accounts of death—death on the highways, death from violent crime, death through war and terrorism, death in plane crashes, and the deaths of older people who had become famous during their lifetime.

In addition to the news accounts of death, TV programs and motion pictures portray violence and death under all kinds of circumstances. Extensive exposure to death in these ways can, of course, leave us untouched. It can make us immune to its impact altogether—until death strikes close to us. We can, if we wish, ignore much of the death around us. But it is also possible for us to use these indirect encounters as an opportunity for interpreting death—and life—as part of God's plan for his world.

There is a great deal of data today which indicates that children are concerned with death and that many children do, in fact, fear death. It is, of course, impossible for us to pinpoint a child's concept of death. Even in a particular child at a particular time, his view of death is not a single thing.

We can gain a general understanding of the stages children experience as their concept of death develops. This can help us. But finally we must rely on our own and the child's sensitivity as we talk about death together.

LISTENING

Being sensitive to children as well as adults means really listening. We always need to ask what truth the child is seeking. For truth is not truth-for-me unless it answers the real question I am asking, unless it speaks to my particular need at this particular moment.

Little Johnny came running into the kitchen. "Mother," he asked, "where did I come from?"

His mother wiped her hands. She had long been expecting this and yet she was apprehensive now that the time had come. She explained how mommies and daddies love each other and plan babies.

She explained, simply and honestly, how babies are born.

When she finally finished, Johnny said, "No, mommy, I mean, Billy came from Chicago. Where did I come from?"

With adults, and especially with children, we need to be continually sensitive to what is *really* being said. One way to do this is to make our answers shorter, to pause more often so the child can respond. Ask yourself how what you are saying is being understood. Give the child frequent opportunities to let you know what he's hearing and whether you are really dealing with what he wants to know.

Listening means hearing the words; but it also means hearing what is behind and between the words that are spoken. "I hate you" may really mean "I feel mean and unlovable." We must try to put ourselves in the child's position if we are really to hear him.

A ten-year-old girl whose mother has died cries out in anger, "I hate you, God." How might you respond? Might you say, "God is love; you must never hate God!"? What would you say? It helps if before we speak we take a few seconds to think about what is really being said. The child is probably saying, "I've never, ever felt so deserted and alone. I'm frightened to death." If this is the real meaning behind her expression of hatred, then the last thing she needs is a lecture on the loving nature of God.

We can test our interpretation by asking questions. For example, "You're feeling scared and alone, aren't you?" If the child's response suggests that anger is the dominant feeling rather than fear or loneliness, we might respond like this: "You've never felt so mad before, have you? Tell me how you feel." Testing our assumptions with questions is an important part of listening.

Touching and holding the child can be as important as the things we say. Listening means responding to the needs of the whole person, not just to the words spoken. It means being accepting rather than judgmental. It means opening ourselves to involvement and the possibility of being hurt. Listening is a form of loving!

FROM THREE TO FIVE

We know that the child's view of death is not logical; it is made up of paradoxes. For example, young children do not conceive of the possibility of their own death. They are bothered, nevertheless, by their knowledge that adults, who are stronger than they are, do die. How, they wonder, can children, who are weaker, survive?

Knowing that a child's view of death is not logical means that factual, rational approaches to questions and fears about death will not always be adequate. To say, "your anger didn't cause Grandpa's death" is true and may need to be said. But saying it won't necessarily make the child's guilt and fear go away.

Empathy, or feeling with the child, is an important ingredient in meeting a child's questions and fears. Just being there—listening to their words and accepting the feelings they express—is more important than any explanation we might give.

Children from the age of three to five tend to see death as something temporary that may come in degrees. We may hear a child say, "I shot you dead, real dead." In the next instant, the dead one can be alive and well and the game goes on. For the young child there is no clear distinction between life and lifelessness.

It is not unusual for a young child who has been taken to his grandpa's funeral to ask later, "Is Grandpa coming to play with me today?" It's not that he has forgotten or that he failed to understand what he was told. Most likely, this question reflects his inability to see death as something final and permanent.

There is no need to take the "don't you remember" or "can't you understand" approach. Our most helpful response would be a factual answer to an honest question: "No, Grandpa won't be coming to play anymore; he died."

Slowly, then, the child's understanding of death develops. We need to provide support and help him find answers. But we must respect each child's rate of growth. Not all children crawl and walk and talk at the same age. There are individual differences. Similarly, developing a concept of death is a process that comes at different rates in different children, depending on each individual child and on that child's life situation and experience.

FROM FIVE TO NINE

From about age five, children gradually begin to accept the fact that death is final, universal, and personal. It is not unusual for a six- or seven-year-old to say as ours once did, "You know, dad, I was thinking on the school bus today that someday you'll die. It will be hard for me when you do." This gradual realization tends to be actualized in most children by the age of nine. Here, again, there is fluctuation. Children shift from expressions of real understanding to less realistic attitudes and back again.

We can help or hinder the growth process depending on how we respond to our children when they bring up subjects relating to death. When our son told us of his thoughts on the school bus I said, "Yes, Peter, it is hard when parents die. I had a big empty feeling when my dad died." Let the conversation move naturally. Don't change the subject when death comes up. That could make the child even more fearful—about something too terrifying even to discuss.

I firmly believe that facing life means we must face the possibility of our own death at any time. This can be accomplished in connection with the necessity for making arrangements for who would rear children if both parents died. Our children know that their godparents would want them and that that is what their mother and daddy want. In the event that we were to die at the same time, at least the uncertainty about "what will happen to me" will not be an added burden for our children. In addition, such advance planning means that the reality of death for all of us is acknowledged. Death is a part of life. We plan for it just as we plan for vacations, for our jobs, for the future.

During the ages of about five to nine, the cause of death is often personified. The child may suffer terrible guilt feelings if, as is often the case, he has expressed anger toward a person who later died. This problem is most acute if it is the child's own parent who has died.

Feelings of guilt and fear are enhanced by the notion that the child's own words or thoughts can cause death. This is especially true if the child is unable to talk about it. It is therefore important for us to help children deal with those feelings. Rabbi Earl Grollman, in a book written for parents and children to read together, approaches the subject like this:

> Are you worried?
> Afraid you did something wrong and
>   that's why grandfather is not here—
>   as a punishment to you?
> OF COURSE NOT![4]

Accepting the child's feelings and helping him accept his own feelings is an important first step in meeting this problem of guilt.

Children may suffer from feelings that their anger caused the death of someone they loved. At the same time, they often feel anger toward the one who died, anger over the fact that they themselves have been abandoned. This anger needs to be expressed. It is important that we not add to the problem by saying "You musn't feel angry towards your mother." On the contrary, without encouraging them to repress any anger which they may feel, we can reassure them that they were loved by the dead person.

RESPONSES TO DEATH

Anna Freud has shown that children learn to love by first loving their mother. It is this relationship to the mother which establishes an extremely important pattern that remains throughout life. If the mother dies, the children may respond in one of several ways.

It is possible that they will remain attached to the dead person in a fantasy world. In order that healing can occur we must help the child face the pain that the real world brings.

They might possibly shift their investment of love from persons to things or activities. We all know people who love *things* and use *persons*—often because they are afraid of additional hurts if they open themselves to loving and being loved by other persons. Somehow we need to help such people experience the joy that can come through loving persons.

It is also possible for the children to be too afraid to reach out in love again to anyone; they may simply turn in on themselves. Those who reach out in love to a child like this are very apt to experience rejection. Yet, it is very important to try and try and try. Professional help may be needed as well.

Finally, we would hope that the children could accept the loss and could respond in love to another person. It is this response which we want to help the children achieve.

The child's understanding of death develops gradually, as we have said. It never remains constant. A child may show a real grasp of the permanency and universality of death one day, then say something the next day which implies that death is temporary. This need not overly concern us. If we can remain open and respond honestly each time the topic of death comes up, the child's concept of death will grow.

Where we are ourselves and where each child is in the growth process determines the starting point of any exploration into the mystery of death. But we must be willing to talk freely about the subject and not back off from it.

It is important to use a normal tone of voice. Avoiding questions, using hushed tones, and giving ever-zealous or overly pious lectures can all communicate an uneasiness about death. Jesus' parable about removing the log out of our own eye before we try to take the speck out of our brother's eye speaks to me at this point. Until I face death and know what I believe, I cannot help others understand and accept death. Each of us must come to terms with the meaning of death—and life!

This certainly does not mean that we have all of the answers; our own understanding of death matures and changes as long as we live. It does mean that we should be secure enough in our own faith and understanding that we can encourage our children to raise questions and to express their real feelings. We need to be accepting and open in our response. "I don't know" is sometimes the only honest answer we can give. When it is, we should not be afraid to use it!

THREE

Pitfalls to Avoid

Let no one deceive you with empty words, for it is because of these things that the wrath of God comes upon the sons of disobedience.

Ephesians 5:6

It should be clear by now that canned answers to a list of questions children ask about death won't work. No one can tell us what to say if truth-for-me and openness to the child are our preferred guidelines. But there are some fairly common approaches that have been shown to be more harmful than helpful. There are some answers we should *not* give.

"SHE'S JUST SLEEPING."

There has been a tendency—almost a passion—in our society to make the dead person appear to be sleeping peacefully. This has sometimes been carried to excess—for example, by propping the corpse up in a bed to be viewed or providing an innerspring casket.

I would suggest that one explanation for this is that as a society we refuse to accept the fact of death. When we tell a child that his aunt is "just sleeping,"

23

we are of course trying simply to soften the pain and grief that death brings. The intent is understandable. But what are we really saying to the child?

The child may then begin to experience fear at bedtime. There is that gnawing realization that Auntie once went to sleep and didn't wake up, and then was put in the ground. Perhaps, the child fears, this time I won't wake up either and they'll put me in the ground too.

What was meant to soften the child's encounter with death can make him afraid to go to sleep. He still has to learn—and cope with—the fact that the dead person is not sleeping and will not wake up. Added to this burden may now be the fear that he himself will go to sleep and not wake up.

Often this fear is in the subconscious. It probably will not be something he understands and can talk about. This makes it even more difficult for us to help the child, when his strongest feelings are so deep-seated.

When we tell a child, "She's just sleeping...," we are really not helping—and could be hurting—the child. Avoiding this approach can help us as we struggle to discover ways of truly helping children face death.

SICK ... HOSPITAL ... DEAD!

Unthinkingly, we can often explain death in such a way that the child sees it as the natural outcome of being seriously ill and confined in a hospital. Without realizing it, we may be reinforcing the child's perception that people who are very sick or who are hospitalized die.

Our response to the child's questions may be honest, simple, and straightforward, but this may not be enough. In addition, we need always to put ourselves in the child's position. What experiences has he had? What context of life helps to shape his interpretation?

If the child has known even one or two people who died while in the hospital, it is reasonable for him to assume that people who go to the hospital die. In the same way, we need to be sensitive to the fact that perhaps the only time we've said, "She's very sick" was shortly before Grandmother's death. What then might our child perceive later on when we say, in truth, "Be quiet, the baby is very sick!"?

We need to be attuned to the experiences a child brings with his questions. Our answers may or may not change as a result of such knowledge and sensitivity. In any event, we may want to provide experiences that will help the child realize that very sick people can and often do get well.

For example, there may be value in having a child wait briefly in a hospital lobby with one parent while the other parent visits a family friend. Later, the child can go along to visit the friend at home. Then when children face hospitalization themselves, or the hospitalization of a parent, they will know that the hospital is a place where people also go to get well, not just a place where some people die.

The key here is to be sensitive to children's previous experience. Then we can be more sensitive to the conclusions they are likely to draw when they plug our answers into their life situation. The way a child faces serious illness or hospitalization can be affected by the relationship which is seen between sickness, hospitals, and death.

"HE'S GONE ON A LONG JOURNEY."

This approach is, at least, misleading for a child. The results toward which it tends are not positive. Instead of lessening the pain death brings, it is apt to raise a whole new set of anxieties: "Why would my mommy desert me?" "Didn't she love me?" "Will she come back?" Whether or not the child actually verbalizes them, the questions are likely to be lurking in that little mind.

Moreover, this approach subtly suggests that death is not final. After all, people do come back from long journeys, don't they? Besides, just what does "long" mean to a three-year-old or a ten-year-old?

In addition, children who have been told that a dead person "has gone on a long journey" often feel real fear whenever they are left by their parents. Perhaps, the child reasons, my mommy and daddy too are leaving on a "long journey."

Studies of children and death have shown that a fear of trips can also develop as a result of this explanation of death. Think about the swirl of events a child experiences at the death of someone who was important to them. Their routine is upset. There is tension in the air. People are upset and crying. Then they are told, "Grandpa went on a long journey." Imagine after all this a child's vision of that journey, and how scary such a trip must seem.

This approach can be downright harmful. What may seem like an innocent half-truth, which we hope will make it easier for the child, can become a wild chase down back roads from one roadblock to another. We owe it to our children to walk the main highway with them—to take the direct route and to share the pain from the bumps as we hit them together!

"GOD NEEDED HER."

This answer arises out of our own frustration and sense of helplessness. When we don't know what else to say, we may be tempted to blame God. It is understandable. But it is wrong and can cause serious problems for the child.

Death can't be explained away by blaming anyone, for death is a part of life. We all die. It is natural. But because we cannot accept untimely death, we often look for someone to blame.

Sometimes we can point to the driver of the other

car, or the drug pusher, or "that incompetent doctor," or the "system." Sometimes, though, there is no one to blame. The doctors did everything they could. Who can be faulted when a child dies of leukemia or a young father dies of a brain tumor? Feeling angry and totally helpless, we can think of nothing else to say to a grieving child except, "God needed your daddy."

I know of no better way to cause a child to feel hostile and angry toward God. "But why," he may think, "did God take my daddy? Doesn't he know I need him?"

This approach reflects a "god-of-the-gaps" understanding. God fills only the gaps not yet filled by human knowledge and learning. Whatever we cannot explain—good or bad—we attribute to him. But this view does violence to a Christian understanding of a loving God who cared so much that he sent Jesus Christ to live and die among us and to conquer the power of death over us.

A middle-aged woman recently told me, "I still feel guilty about how deeply I resented God for taking my father when I was a little girl." The guilt and resentment she has carried for years is a high price to pay for three words spoken out of desperation when she was a child.

When we are at a loss to explain, we need the honesty to say, "I just don't understand why your daddy died." We may even add a simple prayer: "My

God, help me to know and to accept!" But we must avoid saying, "God needed him." Blaming God for something we are unable to understand or accept is a cop-out that can do immense harm to a grieving child.

"GOD PUNISHED HER."

"You know," I heard the lady say, "she had a baby out of wedlock and gave it up for adoption. God is punishing her. That's why her son was run over. That's God's way of punishing her for her sin!"

When I heard this I felt sick. Then I felt sorry for the lady who believed that God acts in such ways. When tragedy strikes her family, I wonder, will she have the added burden of searching her own past for something she may have done that displeased God?

It is easy to fall into this simple trap when death strikes someone we think is evil. But then, what can we say when death strikes a "good person"? How can we know whether or not God acts to punish evildoers by striking them down? Does God use death to punish individuals for their sins?

I believe we must look to the Scriptures for answers to these questions. Nowhere in the New Testament does Jesus judge a person's relationship to God by the time or manner of his death. There are at least two instances where Jesus clearly rejects an attempt to equate death with punishment for sin.

In Luke 13:1–5 we read:

> There were some present at that very time who told him of the Galileans whose blood Pilate had mingled with their sacrifices. And he answered them, "Do you think that these Galileans were worse sinners than all the other Galileans, because they suffered thus? I tell you, No; but unless you repent you will all likewise perish. Or those eighteen upon whom the tower in Siloam fell and killed them, do you think that they were worse offenders than all the others who dwelt in Jerusalem? I tell you, No; but unless you repent you will all likewise perish."

Jesus uses these happenings to call people to repentance. But he clearly states that, contrary to the popular belief of that day, suffering and overwhelming disaster are not to be interpreted as the consequence of sin.

I am convinced that we get ourselves into unnecessary difficulty when we take this approach. We know that the Father "makes his sun rise on the evil and on the good, and sends rain on the just and on the unjust" (Matt. 5:45). It is not our place to decide which is which. Death at a particular time and in a particular manner, Jesus claims, is not the result of one's "goodness" or "badness." We need to avoid any explanation of death which would lead a child to conclude otherwise.

"SO WHAT?"

A nonchalance about death—and life—can also be a problem. I believe we rob both life and death of significant meaning when we take an "I don't give a care" attitude. We need to ask what is really being affirmed and what is really being denied when we adopt the lifestyle characterized by, "Live it up today, for tomorrow we die!"

There are many different ways we can express a callousness toward the loss of human life. For example, it is distressing to me when people are glad because the enemy dead are reported to outnumber our own ten to one, or when a plane crash report assures us that none of our people were aboard. What we believe about death is a good indication of how we value life.

What we believe about war, drinking before driving, capital punishment, abortion, and the right to die should give us insight into our own attitudes about both death and life. To the extent that we are indifferent to death or refuse to assume responsibility for the taking of human life, we render life meaningless and empty.

The Christian faith affirms that death is not to be feared. But neither is life to be taken lightly.

FOUR

When Pets Die

How lovely is thy dwelling place,
  O Lord of hosts!
My soul longs, yea, faints
  for the courts of the Lord;
my heart and flesh sing for joy
  to the living God.
Even the sparrow finds a home,
  and the swallow a nest for herself,
  where she may lay her young,
at thy altars, O Lord of Hosts,
  my king and my God.
Blessed are those who dwell in thy house,
  ever singing thy praise!   *Psalm 84:1–4*

ONE FAMILY'S RESPONSE

Recently I got a call from our veterinarian's office. "Your guinea pig is deceased," she said.

"We'll be after him as soon as the children come home from school," was my reply.

It was a cold, rainy November day when the three of us went after Mr. President. We had often laughed about how he reminded us of Theodore Roosevelt in the film at Mt. Rushmore. Peter, age eight, held the dead weight of our one-year-old guinea pig in his hands and then turned away so no one would see his tears. Kris, age six, looked but didn't want to touch the stiff, cold body.

We brought Mr. President home, dug a grave under the lilac bush at the corner of the garage, and stood in the cold drizzle. We put Mr. President in the hole we had dug and gently covered him with wet, black dirt. As we worked we prayed a remembering kind of prayer.

"Thank you, God, for all the fun we had with Mr. President."

"Remember how he squeaked whenever you opened the refrigerator, mommy?"

"He always wanted a carrot!"

"Remember that time when we were cleaning his cage and he got away from Kris and ran into the fireplace and came out gray instead of black because he was covered with ashes?" We laughed through our tears as we all remembered.

"Remember how we moved him home from Minnesota, and there was no room in the car for our feet but we didn't care because we got to keep Mr. President?"

"Please, God, take care of Mr. President!"

"Now Thomas Jefferson Tigger Cat won't be so lonesome, mommy."

We put a piece of rose quartz we had brought back from the Black Hills on top of the grave and ran in out of the cold. Mr. President had joined two gerbils, a cat, and another guinea pig under the lilac bush.

We had faced the fact squarely—Mr. President was dead. We were sad and we cried. But we laughed too as we remembered funny things about him. We buried him simply, but reverently.

I still remember, though, what the woman at the veterinarian's office said to me: "You'd be surprised how many parents can't bring themselves to tell their children a pet has died. Sometimes they tell them the vet gave their pet to someone else." What, we may ask, does this say to the child about veterinarians, and parents, and truth-telling?

This reminded me of a woman I knew who rushed out to buy a new parakeet while her children were sleeping, so they wouldn't know that their own had died. She missed an important opportunity for helping her children face death. Ignoring death won't work in the long run.

Often a pet's death is the first chance we have to help our children come to terms with the meaning of death. It can be the basis for a healthy, growing understanding of life and death.

But it can also be, as we have seen, the beginning of a deceitful, denying, and dishonest approach to the meaning of death. We dare not let this happen if we want to develop an open and honest atmosphere for exploring the meaning of death with our children.

What we may take to be "kindness" and "sparing them needless heartache at such a young age" is really more harmful than helpful. Speaking the truth in love and sharing the sadness it brings when a pet dies is the best approach in helping a child face life. It is not always easy; but in the long run it is best.

THE TRUTH CAN HURT

Sometimes it's hard to help our children face the truth. When we back the car over the puppy or when the neighbor runs over our cat, it hurts us to hurt our child with the truth. But what are the alternatives and where do they lead?

"The puppy ran away."

"But why? I loved him!"

Is this really less painful? And in the long run, might we not wish we had shared the truth together? I still wonder at the parents who often take this "less painful approach" and then cannot understand when their teen-agers don't level with them. Is it any wonder?

My friend's three-year-old daughter saw her kitten hit on the highway in front of her house. What is one to say to a three-year-old's plea? "But mommy, I know she didn't want to die. She looked right in my eyes and I could tell!"

There isn't much we can say. We can hold the child. We can be there. It's hard! But that is life! And death! Denying or ignoring it won't help.

The man who hit the kitten stopped. He was distraught to see the child so upset. He apologized, though it wasn't really his fault. And then, because he felt so helpless standing there with a mother he didn't know, a sobbing child, and a dead kitten, he gave the child fifty cents, patted her on the arm, and left.

I could not fault this stranger who cared enough to stop; at least he did *something* at a time when he did not know what to do or say. But neither did I know how to answer the mother when she asked me, "What could I reply when my daughter looked up at me and said, 'Why did that man pay me to kill my kitty?' "

Sometimes it hurts a lot to be truthful when a child's pet dies. But facing death as a part of life and sharing the burden of sadness can provide a solid foundation for the child's developing attitude toward life and death.

Our job is to help children face the fact of death. This means we must also help them work through any feelings of guilt or resentment they might feel.

The child might be angry with himself—"If only I'd called Bouncer in when daddy told me to. It's my fault." He might feel resentment toward the neighbor—"Why did dumb old Mrs. Brown run over my kitty. She's just a mean old lady." At such a time of loss and anger we need to love the child, accept his feelings, and help him gradually work them through.

Painful though it is, a pet's death can provide the opportunity for developing a healthy and accepting attitude toward death. To deny children this confrontation with death and to refuse to help them meet the situation in truth will cripple them later when they cannot escape the reality of the death of someone they love.

ANSWERING HARD QUESTIONS

I would be less than truthful if I did not admit that once we opt for the "face death in truth" approach, we're bound to be asked some hard questions. Children have a way of going right to the heart of the issue.

Let me share some simple guidelines I have found helpful in answering children's questions—on any subject. You may want to alter them for yourself or come up with an entirely different list. But I am convinced that guidelines are the key. Never in a million years can we anticipate the questions children ask! There's no way we can be prepared with all the answers! Our only hope is to have some principles at hand to guide us when the hard questions are asked.

Be accepting. Any question, honestly asked, deserves a serious answer.

Be honest. I try never to give an answer that I can't accept and believe.

Be straightforward. I try to answer the question that is asked as simply as possible. Then stop. If the child wants more information, he'll ask.

Don't lecture. This is one of the most difficult

guidelines for me to follow. It's all too tempting to
make a point or to moralize.

Say "I don't know" when you don't know. This, of
course, can be a cop-out unless you're willing to help
the child try to find an answer. A teacher I once knew
recommended, "If you don't know, bluff!" But this is
never helpful and can destroy relationships almost
beyond repair.

These guidelines are often easier to repeat than to
implement. How they can actually operate may become clear in the illustration that follows. My
answers obviously will be different from yours. My
purpose here is simply to illustrate a method that,
appropriately adapted, can be used to answer difficult questions.

The question comes! "But, mommy, will Bouncer
go to heaven?"

Guidelines flash—accepting . . . honest . . .
straightforward. . . . Then I answer: "I don't really
know. But I do believe that God will do whatever is
best for Bouncer." Now I have to remind myself—
and even fight—to avoid lecturing. What I've said is
not enough—for me. I'm not ready to stop but, hopefully, I will.

I've answered the question. If the child is satisfied, that is good. If not, she may continue, "But how
do you know that, mommy?"

"Well, Jesus once told his disciples that God
knows and cares about the sparrows. I believe God

cares about everything in his world. He cares about you and he cares about Bouncer too. I trust God to do whatever is best for Bouncer."

"But, mommy, will Bouncer go to heaven?"

"I don't know, honey."

Now if you really believe Bouncer will go to heaven, then, by my guidelines, you should say so. But if you don't, then saying, "Yes, sure, honey!" may seem easier at the moment, but it's potentially more harmful than helpful. There's lots more at stake than just sadness because Bouncer died.

Think about this. In the long run you are either saying "Yes, you can trust me to answer your questions honestly" or you are saying "You can see that I'll tell you whatever is easiest at the moment." The approach we adopt—the guidelines we choose to follow—will have a long-term effect on our relationship with our children as they mature.

FIVE

Helping a Child When Death Comes

Finally, all of you, have unity of spirit, sympathy, love of the brethren, a tender heart and a humble mind.   *1 Peter 3:8*

KNOW WHAT YOU BELIEVE

As adults we will be called on to face death with children. They may be our sons or daughters, nieces or nephews, grandchildren, students, friends, or neighbors. Whatever the time or place, our attitudes toward death will deeply influence theirs. Pre-programmed answers to anticipated questions will not do!

This means that it is important to take time first—in advance—to reflect on our own beliefs about death. A tool that might help in the process is completing these sentences:

1) Death is . . .
2) Dying . . .
3) Talking about death . . .
4) To me, resurrection . . .
5) Heaven . . .
6) Hell . . .

7) Death and life . . .

8) A funeral . . .

Once you have done this, think about your answers. Were they personal or impersonal? Why? Can you live—and even die—with your answers? For you did the exercise raise more questions than it answered?

Do you see death as an enemy—as something to be denied and defied? For many people material goods and services have become centrally important. Our efforts focus on education, achievement, social acceptance. They have become our gods. These goals and prizes all presuppose that man is in control of his own fate and of the world. In such a context, death may well be seen as ultimate failure, because it cuts people off from that which they value most highly.

Accordingly, death must be denied. We spend millions on medical research to defy and defeat it. We protect ourselves from death's presence. Death generally does not take place in the home, in the midst of loved ones. More often it occurs in hospitals or in homes for the aged. We tend to keep our children away from encounters with the dying and to dodge the questions children ask. If we see death as a thief, taking from us all that we value most highly, then we will certainly regard it as something horrible and ugly, and will seek to avoid it.

Do you see death simply as the biological end to biological life—nothing more and nothing less?

Think about the implications of this attitude. What does it say for you about the meaning of life?

Perhaps you view death as a mystery—a mystery that can be understood only as one becomes fully immersed in life, participating in the total life process. If so, how might you complete those eight sentences? That is the stance from which I began my pilgrimage.

Later in this book, I will share some of my theological thoughts about the meaning of death. But my pilgrimage cannot be yours. It can only suggest, perhaps raise a few questions, and occasionally even provide a new insight. But only you can find your answers.

It is important that you do this first, before the fact. Take time to reflect and to pray. Then when you are confronted with the need to help children you can draw upon your own understanding, faith, and hope. You can try to meet the child's needs, not just your own.

BEGIN WHERE THE CHILD IS

Chances are, if the child you seek to help has encountered death, he or she is not seeking a philosophical or theological answer to the mystery. The first task is to find out how the child perceives and feels about what has happened.

As we have already said, listening is basic. What the child *perceives* will not necessarily be what did, in fact, occur. Remember, for instance, my friend's little girl, who perceived that the man paid her to let him kill her kitten. To listen means to tune in to the person, not just to the words. This is *not* the time to try to change perceptions.

Posing questions may help us to discover where the child is. We might begin by saying, "Tell me about it" or "How do you feel?" Feelings are very important. Does the child feel angry? Abandoned? Guilty? Afraid? Left out? Confused? Try to understand exactly how she feels and why.

Be there with the child. Attend to all the cues, verbal and nonverbal. Be accepting and loving—feeling with the child. This is the first step in helping a child face death. Being there and caring are the key.

MEET INDIVIDUAL NEEDS

Often, the bereaved child will have a distorted view of the real cause of death. There may be terrible guilt feelings and perhaps feelings of anger. Encourage the child to express real feelings. Avoid statements that are judgmental: "You musn't say that!" "Don't feel that way!" However well intended, such comments stifle the expression of feeling. We must accept the way the child feels. Then we can try to help the child see it and accept it too.

We may be able to help the child clarify his feelings by responding with questions. For example,

"You are worried, then, because you got angry with mommy and you think that is why she died?"

We must not gloss over the situation by denying the importance of angry feelings. It would not be helpful to say, "Your mommy knew you didn't mean it." The child would be troubled by such a falsehood. He knows he was, in fact, angry with mommy, and he also knows mommy most certainly knew he was angry.

One could perhaps say, "We are sorry when we make others unhappy. Sometimes I make you unhappy, don't I?" (Allow time to talk about it together.) "Yet you forgive me and still love me even when I make you angry. Mommy forgave you. She loved you very much. You didn't make her die. All people die."

Another child's feeling-level response may be "I'm angry at mother because she left me alone and I don't know what to do." In response to angry feelings of this sort one might say, "You feel angry that your mother died, don't you?" Anger is not an uncommon response to death. It grows out of feelings of helplessness, feelings that need to be acknowledged, not buried!

We need to listen intently for such feelings and respond with compassion and understanding. Most important, we need to *be there* to help the child struggle with those deep feelings and hurts that are uniquely his or her own.

CONFRONT REALITY

It is important to begin with a simple but factual explanation for the death encountered. We might say, "She was old and her body was worn out." This, of course, is the easiest kind of death to accept and to explain.

But how might we explain the death of a child or the death of a family killed by a drunken driver? What can we say about the victims of war and natural disaster?

Again, guidelines can help keep us heading in the direction we want to go. Applying my own guidelines to these situations means that I must be accepting, honest, and straightforward; I must not moralize, and I must admit it when I don't know the answer to a specific question.

Many people die of heart disease today. When someone dies of a heart attack, we may explain that "his heart wore out and stopped working." Language like "God struck him down in the prime of life!" doesn't explain death; rather it complicates the issue and raises unnecessary problems with which the child will have to deal. Begin with a factual explanation of the reason death occurred.

When a child dies of leukemia we may say, "Jimmy had a blood disease that we don't know how to cure. Someday perhaps we will learn how to help everyone with that disease." What is needed is an honest and simple statement of what happened.

What can one say when neighbors are killed by a drunken driver? "The man who hit their car had been drinking and was driving too fast." In some cases, of course, we may not know what caused the accident. Then all we can say is, "They were in a bad accident and were killed."

How can we explain why someone we cared for died in a war? This is a difficult problem. We need to avoid statements like, "The Communists killed him!" War is much too complex to blame any one person or group. My own response might be, "We feel sad that Bob was shot. When men try to solve their problems by fighting wars, many people die. We are sorry about all of the people who are killed in war."

Natural disasters are often the most difficult for us to explain. The temptation to blame God is great. Our world is governed by laws of nature. Sometimes we don't understand them, but sometimes we ignore them. Perhaps we can say, "We know if we didn't have earthquakes the earth would explode. The earthquake had to happen, but we are sorry for the people who died in it."

Sometimes we can only answer, "I don't know." But in facing death and the questions it raises we must always begin with simple, honest answers.

The reality of death forces us to make arrangements for the funeral and burial. I think that children, at least by age five, should participate in the services for the dead. They should also be prepared ahead of time for what will take place.

When my father died Peter was five and Kristin was three. Word of his death came when the children were with a babysitter. When we got home Peter was visibly upset—"because Grandpa died" and because "Kris isn't even upset."

We tried to involve the children in our preparations and to share our sorrow with them even as we shared it with the other adults in our family. While we planned to take Peter and Kristin to the funeral and commital service, I did not plan to take them to view the body (an error on my part, I now think). But Peter was insistent that he wanted to "see Grandpa's body." So my mother, my husband, and I took him into the chapel to view the body.

I have known several adults with real hang-ups about death because as children they had been urged to kiss the corpse of a deceased relative. Now I found myself feeling hesitant and ill at ease, wondering about my child there at the open casket.

How much we can learn from our children if we will only let them follow their own feelings! Peter folded his arms on the edge of the casket and rested his chin on his arms. He stood quietly, looking at his grandfather's body. When he reached out to touch his grandpa's hand, I had to restrain my impulse to stop him.

"Grandpa doesn't feel the way I thought he

would," Peter commented. A few moments later he observed, "He has his train tie pin on because he loved trains. . . (pause) . . . This is just his body. His spirit is with God."

I stood, watching my five-year-old son experience the reality that his grandpa had died. Grandpa's body was in a box and we would put it in a grave but his spirit was with God. Peter was not at all uncomfortable in the presence of the corpse, but he was sad—a tear slipped down his cheek.

Just then, the men from the funeral home asked us to leave so they could close the casket. I was ready to leave but Peter wanted to watch the procedure. We let him. He even helped straighten a corner of the pall, then said to me as they began to move the casket into the sanctuary, "I'm going to the front of the church with Grandpa's body."

Peter's encounter with death was not frightening for him. I believe one important factor was that, apart from indicating that we would all attend the funeral, we let him set his own limits. Viewing and touching the body were neither encouraged nor forbidden. We let him share in our sorrow and grief and we tried to answer his questions.

"Mommy, why are you crying?" deserves more than, "Don't bother mommy. She's upset!" I held Kris close and told her I was crying because I loved my dad and I would miss him very much. But I also told her that Grandpa didn't hurt anymore and he didn't feel bad anymore about not being able to talk. I was glad that Grandpa was with God but I was sad for me—and for Peter and her because now they couldn't play with Grandpa and he couldn't come to visit us.

Kristin, who was three then, says she can't remember either Grandpa or the funeral. But I am still glad we took her with us. Sharing sorrow and supporting one another as a family is, I believe, preferable to leaving a little one out because she is too young to understand.

Letting children participate in the funeral of a loved one is one way to help them confront the reality of death. I think it is good to take children to the funeral of a family friend even if the deceased was not known well. This provides an additional opportunity to help them understand death.

SHARE HOPE

For Christians, accepting and communicating the fact of death is only the first step. We also want to share our faith and hope. And it is imperative that the faith and hope we share is actually *ours*—that we believe it and live by it! "Christian answers" that are not our own answers will only confuse the child and hinder his ability to accept death and to grow in the love of God.

The question of death cannot be separated from the question of meaning in life. The Christian finds the answer to both questions in Jesus Christ—God's eternal love, which entered history through a manger, encountered death on a cross, and overcame death through resurrection so that we might have eternal life.

The Christian is able to accept death openly and without fear when he is able to affirm with Paul "that neither death, nor life, nor angels, nor principalities, nor things present, nor things to come, nor powers, nor height, nor depth, nor anything else in all creation, will be able to separate us from the love of God in Christ Jesus our Lord" (Rom. 8:38).

If the funeral service is a Christian celebration of life in the midst of death, the facing of reality and the sharing of hope merge into one experience. The planning of a service can be a meaningful expression of both the reality of death and a victorious faith in Jesus Christ.

The sharing of Christian hope, however, does not mean the ignoring of pain, grief, and loss—these too Christians feel. Rather, it means being honest about them, sharing them with fellow believers, and upholding each other in love. It means rejoicing that God loves and sustains and keeps us all, now and always.

The sharing is not primarily verbal. The most effective way to communicate to our children the hope that sustains us in the face of death is to live it as we love and support them—and let them express their love and support for us. This is one time when we must not allow the details of living to keep us too busy to love and be loved! It is a time when our very bearing and being can testify to that unique hope we share with the Christians of every age: "Praise be to the God and Father of our Lord Jesus Christ, who in his great mercy gave us new birth into a living hope by the resurrection of Jesus Christ from the dead!" (1 Pet. 1:3 NEB).

A letter we once received expresses beautifully the way in which, for the Christian, sorrow and loss can be so permeated by hope and joy as to give meaning to life and to death:

> Dear friends,
>
> It is not easy for me to write this letter. Yet I value your friendship, and since you are my friends, I want to share with you what has happened.
>
> While walking home with her big sister on December 23, the last day of school before Christmas vacation, our middle child, Andrea, was struck by a car. Miraculously, even though she was holding Andrea's hand, Jennifer escaped injury. Andrea, after emergency surgery and what seemed like an encouraging prognosis, died on Christmas morning. She would have been five on December 30.
>
> How can I communicate to you the beauty there is in sorrow? The concept of "community" has taken on a whole new meaning for me in the crisis of losing Andrea. So many people have reached

out in so many ways—and never before have I been so able to accept my own need for those others who have been there with me in the pain, the joy, and the sadness of all we have gone through together. Indeed, we have held and supported each other in untold new ways.

We had a beautiful service for Andrea—the formulation of which was a struggle for the group of friends we asked to help us with this. It began with a tape of music she loved—children's folk songs by Pete Seeger, Mr. Rogers, and other music—accompanied by slides we had of her, many of them taken by a very close friend—whose own unexpected death preceded Andrea's by only one month and whose spirit freed us to plan the service as we did. Indeed, our closeness to his family during the loss was our own first experience of the beauty that can be found in sorrow, and of the support of community that gave us great strength in dealing with our own loss.

"A Story about Jesus" was a children's book our friend had given Andrea, which told simply of Jesus as a friend of little children. After our pastor's brief message, we prayed the Lord's Prayer. Then we had a moment for sharing together our memories of Andrea—we all remember many things which we treasure—those nearly five years we had together were beautiful ones. During the singing of "The Lord of the Dance" which Andrea loved to dance to—she knew the chorus and we often sang it together—persons at the service were free to join us at the front of the sanctuary and to reach out to each other if they felt free to.

And many persons who were strangers to each other found themselves drawn into an expression of community which was so strongly felt at that moment. It was a moment, an experience, a feeling I shall treasure always. Truly there is beauty in grief which can be shared in such a way. . . .

So it was that one family within their own Christian community was able to live out in an honest way both their grief and their hope.

Their experience is recounted here not to provide a model for others but merely to suggest that each of us is called to find comparable expressions of our own faith and hope, particularly as we confront death. When Christians open themselves and freely share their hurt and their hope, healing results. And I believe this healing is the gift of a loving God.

SIX

Sharing Our Faith

> For God so loved the world that he gave his only
> Son, that whoever believes in him should not
> perish but have eternal life. For God sent the Son
> into the world, not to condemn the world, but that
> the world might be saved through him.
>
> *John 3:16–17*

DEATH: PROBLEM OR MYSTERY?

The society in which we find ourselves is deeply
troubled about its approach to death. It has even
been described as death-denying and death-defying.
And we are very much a part of this society. We tend
to blame death on people or events—ignoring the
fact that we too will die. All people will die, but there
is always that desperate hope that, once medicine
masters cancer and heart disease and transplant
techniques, man will finally be in control.

At the same time, however, members of the church
know that we are a Christian community called into
being and sustained by the gospel. We hear the gospel's assertion that "unless a grain of wheat falls into
the earth and dies, it remains alone; but if it dies, it
bears much fruit" (John 12:24).

The good news is that, like the grain of wheat, we do not stand alone. We need not struggle to be self-sufficient or to live by our own resources alone. Death does not always have to be seen as a problem to be solved. It is rather a mystery, a mystery which can be understood only as we become involved in life, living it to the fullest.

The agonizing question the Christian must face is this: How can we acknowledge the finality of death and at the same time witness to our faith in the resurrection? How can we resolve the apparent contradiction between the cemetery we see and the heaven we do not see except by faith? Can we live with the tension between the two? How can we communicate our understanding of death and life to children, and still leave them free to search for meaning and truth in their own lives?

WHAT IS THE KEY?

What we believe about Jesus determines what we will believe about death—and life. Once again, the completion of open-ended sentences may help to focus ideas and beliefs. This tool can be effective, however, only if we are honest with ourselves:

1) Jesus . . .
2) Jesus' death . . .
3) Jesus' resurrection . . .
4) The difference Jesus makes in my life . . .
5) What I don't understand about Jesus . . .

6) I am bothered by . . .

7) I wish I believed . . .

8) Most central to my faith is . . .

As Christians, we participate in the death of Christ throughout our lives, first through baptism and holy communion and finally in our physical death. Accordingly, death itself is transformed. It is no longer a problem for us to master but a mystery that points to eternal life.

Reuel Howe points out that "men fear death as they fear loneliness, meaninglessness, and non-being." We all want the reassurance that we need not be afraid. There are no blueprints of heaven, no maps for getting there, but says Howe, "God has given us Someone who will meet us there. We know Him. His name is Jesus. We call Him Christ our Lord."[5] Jesus promised us in John 14:3, "When I go and prepare a place for you, I will come again and will take you to myself, that where I am you may be also." Christian hope is rooted in the mystery of Jesus Christ—in his death and resurrection.

Belief in the resurrection does not mean that death has become painless. Death is connected with real suffering and anguish—as it was for the One we call Lord. Although it is now a part of life as we experience it, it was not, according to the writer of Genesis, a part of God's original plan for his world. Fear of death came into being as judgment, as a punishment for man's desire to live by his own rules. Death came as a limitation on man, because of his refusal to live in harmonious relationship with God and other men.

Paul claims in Romans 6:23 that "the wages of sin is death." Human beings fear death not because they are human, but because they are rebel-human. Death is seen as an enemy because of man's sinful nature. All human beings share this rebellious nature. Therefore, we all must personally confront this last enemy, death.

But God is not merely a just God. He is also a God of grace. He saves us from what we rightly deserve. "The last enemy to be destroyed," says Paul, "is death" (1 Cor. 15:26). That enemy, however, has been overcome by Jesus Christ. "The wages of sin is death, but the free gift of God is eternal life in Christ Jesus our Lord" (Rom. 6:23).

Christian hope, then, is the corollary of our belief that Jesus died and rose again. As death points to destruction and the end of life on this earth, so resurrection points toward transformation and the beginning of perfect life in the kingdom of God. Resurrection is not to be seen as an instantaneous something that happens with a "zap" at death. Rather, resurrection begins at baptism, where we die with Christ and are raised a new creature. Resurrection means an ongoing transition from life here on earth toward our eternal life with God. It characterizes life in the present, not just in the future. It is not only a hope but an experienced reality.

Do you not know that all of us who have been baptized into Christ Jesus were baptized into his death? We were buried therefore with him by baptism into death, so that as Christ was raised from the dead by the glory of the Father, we too might walk in newness of life.

For if we have been united with him in a death like his, we shall certainly be united with him in a resurrection like his. We know that our old self was crucified with him so that the sinful body might be destroyed, and we might no longer be enslaved to sin. For he who has died is freed from sin. But if we have died with Christ, we believe that we shall also live with him. For we know that Christ being raised from the dead will never die again; death no longer has dominion over him. The death he died he died to sin, once for all, but the life he lives he lives to God. So you also must consider yourselves dead to sin and alive to God in Christ Jesus.   (Rom. 6:3–11)

WHAT ABOUT BODY AND SOUL?

The idea that body and soul separate from one another at death has caused many difficulties in the Christian understanding of death. Much has been written on the subject and many misconceptions prevail. One thing seems clear to me: the reality to which the idea points is, again, not a problem to be solved but a mystery, part of the mystery of death.

In the novel, *A Canticle for Leibowitz*, we find one expression of this mystery: "Abbot Zerchi smiled thinly. 'You don't *have* a soul, Doctor. You *are* a soul. You have a body temporarily.' "[6] On the other hand, Bishop John A. T. Robinson has said, "Man does not *have* a body, he *is* a body." Robinson sees the body as the outward form of the soul.[7]

The ancient Hebrew understanding, expressed in the Old Testament, never suggested that body and soul are separate and detachable. Our current understanding of gestalt psychology supports this view that a clear distinction between them cannot be made. The human being is, in fact, body-soul. Perhaps it was because of this scriptural belief in the wholeness of man that the church from the very beginning has insisted on speaking of the resurrection of the body:

> So is it with the resurrection of the dead. What is sown is perishable, what is raised is imperishable. It is sown in dishonor, it is raised in glory. It is sown in weakness, it is raised in power. It is sown a physical body, it is raised a spiritual body. If there is a physical body, there is also a spiritual body. (1 Cor. 15:42–44)

The spiritual cannot be seen apart from the material world in which we live. Resurrection means that the whole man is saved by God's grace. It means that the material world is intimately bound up with the eternal. All that is real and of value in life has eternal meaning and value.

Resurrection, I repeat, doesn't happen in a flash. It is a process involving man's participation in the mystery of Christ. The road to resurrection involves man's conscious response to, and creative sharing in, God's promise for meaningful life—for eternal life.

Having said this, though, we are still faced with the problem of explaining to children why we put bodies in the ground, cover them with six feet of dirt, and then say that the person just buried is with God. I have not found any way to talk about this without distinguishing between body and spirit.

Some years ago, shortly after I began teaching in the church school, one of my five-year-olds asked me out of the clear blue, "Mrs. Vogel, what happens to people when they die?"

"We bury their body in the ground," I replied, "but their spirit goes to be with God."

"What's spirit, Mrs. Vogel?"

Who says teaching children is easy? I certainly hadn't anticipated a question like this. But it was an honest question and it needed an answer.

"Spirit is that part of you that is happy and sad and that loves. Does your big toe ever feel happy?"

"No," followed by a giggle.

"We don't need our big toe or any of this body when we die but everything about us that cares and knows and loves goes to be with God."

I make no claim that this is a particularly good answer. I share it only because it was, for me, an honest answer, one that is consistent with the guidelines I subsequently chose to follow.

WHAT IS ETERNAL LIFE?

Much of our talk about the future implies that it goes on forever. We speak of the "hereafter" and of life "after" death. But this is not biblical language. "I am the Alpha and the Omega, the beginning and the end" (Rev. 21:6) points the Christian way.

We may speak of the future somewhat imperfectly, in time-bound images—the only kind we have—but we must not be deceived into thinking that those images are the reality to which they point. Eternity is a different dimension of time—God's "time."

An illustration can perhaps help us to grasp this difference: An hour is an hour—60 minutes, 3600 seconds—right? Yes, but is it? Compare the anguished hour you spend outside the emergency room in which your injured child lies with the delightful hour spent doing your favorite thing with your favorite person. Notice the difference!

I have to admit that while I confess my faith in eternal life I cannot precisely describe that life. For me it is enough to know that it is God's life, the life he is and has and lovingly bestows. And I trust him. I can claim only —but with certainty—that eternal life is the gift of a loving God who values persons. Eternal life is a mystery that I experience in part now, and whose fullness I await in joyful expectation.

WHAT ABOUT HEAVEN AND HELL?

We cannot avoid asking how heaven and hell fit into this understanding of eternal life. We live in an age when many contend that the ideas of heaven and hell are no longer meaningful. Edwin Shneidman reports these findings from a questionnaire about death:

> The typical childhood conception of death is in terms of an afterlife, which for most involves ideas of heaven and hell (57%). But by adulthood, the percentages of individuals who believe in an afterlife as their primary view of death has been cut almost in half to 30%. From late adolescence on, the largest single percentage see death simply as the final process of life (35%).[8]

At the same time there seems to be a resurgence of interest in heaven, hell, and the second coming among Jesus people and many others in our society.

We get off on the wrong foot whenever we assume that heaven and hell are literally places where the dead go. Yet for the Christian, the words "heaven" and "hell" point to a certain reality.

There are times when the most adequate way we can describe an experience is to say "it was hell!" Other times we may say, "I was in seventh heaven!" What are we really saying?

Hell seems an appropriate word when we have a sense of everything being wrong. We are out of relationship with others; we feel like God isn't there or doesn't care; we are alienated from him and from people, and the more we deplore our situation the more we turn in upon ourselves. Christian language refers to this as sin. To say "it's hell" is really to say we are overpowered by sin. Hell has been defined as shutting God out forever.

At other times, we feel all is right with our world. We open ourselves to others and are able to give freely rather than seek for ourselves. We feel at one with people and with God. Integration has overcome alienation. We are able to know God and to accept his love. Our biblical heritage traditionally uses the word "grace" to describe this.

The Christian knows that sin and grace are realities in human life. Each person experiences them both at various times and in varying degrees. The words "heaven" and "hell" point to the reality of sin and grace in man's life in the present, and to the way in which man is able or not able after he dies to participate in eternal life with God.

Heaven, then, is not primarily a place. We can be misled by images of gold streets and harpists with wings. Heaven is an eternal relationship we have with God and other people, a relationship made possible because of God's forgiving love, whereby he grants us participation in the mystery of Christ's death and resurrection.

So we can say to our children, "We miss Grandpa

but we can be glad Grandpa doesn't hurt or feel sad anymore. His body is in the ground. But all that loved and was loved in Grandpa is with God and we believe God will love him and care for him in a way more beautiful and more wonderful than we can imagine. When people say Grandpa is in heaven this is what we mean."

Hell is not a place either. Images of fiery furnaces and red-suited devils complete with horns, tails, and pitchforks may cause people to fear or ridicule God, but they do not help us discover the meaning of hell. I find the most satisfactory understanding of hell to be one that involves relationship—it is hell when a person is cut off from eternal life and the presence of God's love, when people are so self-centered that they are unable to receive the loving gift of eternal life with God.

If we would be honest with our children, we can never say of another person, "She went to hell." We can only portray hell as the final lot of those who reject God's gift of forgiveness, life, and love. Who these people are he knows; we do not.

In the final analysis, heaven and hell remain symbols which point to a truth. But that truth is clothed in mystery. I believe we need to use images which speak to us in our human situation. But we must never forget that our images are not the reality to which they point. Heaven and hell are a part of the mystery of death.

HOW DO WE SHARE ALL THIS WITH A CHILD?

I believe that by the time children are five they are ready to hear a simple telling of the Holy Week and Easter stories. They can begin to understand the hosannas of Palm Sunday, the conversation of Jesus' last supper with his friends, the cruel crucifixion, and the joy Jesus' friends felt when they found the tomb empty and discovered that Jesus was still alive!

But it is obvious that we can't sit children down, read to them from Romans and Corinthians, and expect them to have acquired a Christian understanding of death. How, then, can we begin to lay the foundation for Christian growth?

First, we need to come to the point in our own Christian development where this understanding is real and operative in our lives. Then in our daily living we will communicate to our children the fact that they are loved very much—God loves us all, adults and children, even when we make wrong choices. His love does not depend on our prior good behavior. This is the heart of the good news, and it can be shared even with very young children by the way we relate to them. This is an important beginning for their Christian growth.

We can also live out our beliefs whenever we face a death experience with our children—be it the death of a pet, a wild animal, or a person. Children can sense our acceptance and faith—or our anger and resentment—in the way we meet such situations.

Our actions communicate more than anything we might say or not say. In fact, before we ever utter a word, we begin communicating our deepest feelings. The expression on our faces, the sound of our voices when we speak, the questions we try to avoid, all provide our children with feelings and concepts for understanding—or misunderstanding—death.

Knowing where we stand—and what we believe—frees us to answer questions the child may ask from where he stands. But, I repeat, there is no need to give rational, logical answers to deeply-*felt* questions until such time as the child is old enough and ready to hear and consider and discuss them.

Death is a reality which all human beings must face—no one escapes it. Death is also a mystery—the faith of the Christian enables him to face it head on. All die, but Jesus Christ is the victor over death. For "God shows his love for us in that while we were yet sinners Christ died for us" (Rom. 5:8). The Christian is able to rejoice with Paul that "death is swallowed up in victory. . . . Thanks be to God who gives us the victory through our Lord Jesus Christ" (1 Cor. 15:54b–57).

Perhaps we can pray with Michel Quoist:

> People were following:
> The family—some crying,
> Some pretending to cry;
> Friends—some grieving,
> Some bored or chatting.

Leaving the cemetery, some of the family were sobbing: All is finished.

Others were sniffling: "Come, come my dear, courage: it's finished!"

Some friends murmured: "Poor man, that's how we'll all finish."

And others sighed in relief: "Well, it's finished."

And I was thinking that everything was just beginning.

Yes, he has finished the last rehearsal, but the play was just beginning.

———   ———   ———

The years of training were over, but the eternal work was about to start.

He had just been born to life,

The real life,

Life that's going to last,

Life eternal.

———   ———   ———

Death, grotesque character, bogey-man of little children, non-existent phantom,

I don't take you seriously. But I am disgusted with you.

You terrify the world,

You frighten and deceive men,

And yet your only reason for existing is Life, and you are not able to take from us those that we love.

Lord, I love you, and I want to love you more.

It's you who makes love eternal, and I want to love eternally.[9]

Let it be!

SEVEN

Where Do We Go from Here?

I believe; help my unbelief !   *Mark 9:24*

"So," you say, "I have to be honest with my children. But what then am I supposed to do? I have a real problem about death. I want to accept death but . . . !"

That is a fair question. And there are some things adults can do to grow in their own understanding of death and dying.

PRAY

This is the most important advice I can give. But I am aware that it may sound like the biggest cop-out of the century. I know, because for agonizing months I felt like my prayers were bouncing off the ceiling. But I also know that when I was finally able to accept death, my very acceptance was itself a gift from God—an answer to those prayers I felt he had not been hearing.

Prayer is an important expression of our relationship with God. The thing that keeps me praying when I feel like my prayers are futile is my belief that God's hearing is not dependent on how I feel.

Even when it seems like God doesn't care, we must continue praying because of Jesus' promise: "Ask, and it will be given you; seek, and you will find; knock, and it will be opened to you. For every one who asks receives, and he who seeks finds, and to him who knocks it will be opened" (Matt. 7:7–8).

Even though the words we use do not make a lot of difference, formulating our prayers can often be helpful. I have found that sometimes the very struggle to put my questions and doubts into words can turn out to be the vehicle God uses to show me new insights.

Neglecting to verbalize our prayers can lead away from a meaningful prayer life. We may reason that, since God knows anyway, I don't need to put my prayers into words. But soon our openness to God's will is forgotten because we have become too busy trying to solve all of our problems ourselves.

What is vitally important is that we remain open to God's leading—that we look to him for guidance and strength. He speaks to us in many different ways if we will only discipline ourselves and take the time to focus on what he is saying to us in the life situation where we are. Prayer is an important link in maintaining our relationship with him.

READ

New insights often come to us through what we read. Good books can open up new worlds for us. Once again, I find guidelines helpful.

Try to really understand what the writer means. Often we quarrel with a writer over particular sentences or words, while failing to understand his basic position. I knew a teacher once who said, "I'll listen to why you think the author is wrong *after* you tell me what the author says." There is much to be learned from this approach.

Be open to new ideas. It is important to approach a subject from many different viewpoints. We cheat ourselves and limit the channels through which God can speak to us when we read only materials that reflect our own ideas and biases.

Engage in dialogue with the writer. Your own convictions are important too. Ask yourself: "Do I agree with that?" "Why or why not?" "What does the author mean by that?" "How would I say it differently?"

Be selective in what you appropriate. Rarely is any writer all right or all wrong. Accept what rings true for you. Withhold judgment in those areas where you need more evidence or time to think. Try to evaluate fairly and—by disagreeing or by agreeing —to learn.

Seek advice on what to read. In this connection I would recommend the following books as good beginning points:

Elizabeth Kubler-Ross's *On Death and Dying* explains the five stages of dying. The author uses many case studies. Her book is clearly written and

easy to understand. ...
for dying persons an...
sons. Since that inclu...
read it the better.

Nathan A. Scott has e...
Death which has some
Among them are "The Ti
Joseph Matthews and "Th
Tillich.

Fiction often grapples serio   ...ning
of life and death. There are ma   ...ooks in this
category from which to choose.

Leo Tolstoy wrote *The Death of Ivan Ilych* in
Russia in 1886. His insight into human nature is
fascinating as he deals with the ways people cope
with death and dying. The book is a classic well
worth reading and rereading.

For those who lean toward science fiction, Walter
M. Miller, Jr., has written *A Canticle for Leibowitz*,
a commentary on the inability of the human race to
learn from its past mistakes. It presents life-death
decisions in the context of conflicts between religion
and society. It is a thought-provoking book, to say the
least.

My family's favorite books are *The Chronicles of
Narnia* by C. S. Lewis, a boxed set of seven paper-
backs. The first book in the series is *The Lion, the
Witch, and the Wardrobe*. These are children's
books that the whole family can enjoy. The author

ggle between good and evil—
and death—in such a way that once
ading you probably won't be able to stop.
bibliography at the back of this book contains
ther suggestions about books worth reading.
Good books can be of tremendous help as you struggle to find meaning in your own life.

KEEP A LOG

Keeping a log or diary can be a real help as we
struggle to find meaning for life and to accept death.
We should write down our innermost thoughts,
frustrations, doubts, and questions. You may share
whatever you want to from it, of course, but a log is
private. It is personal. No one should expect you to
divulge its contents.

In addition to your own thoughts, write down new
ideas that come from your reading or from your
conversations with others. Children often put things
together in fresh ways. When they do, jot it down.
Sometimes a line or phrase from a movie, TV program, or comic strip gives food for thought; write it
down.

The log will help you take some time for yourself.
You may sit down to write and end up just thinking.
That's fine! You probably wouldn't have taken the
time if it hadn't been for that log.

In a log of this kind spelling and sentence struc-
ture are unimportant. The purpose is to focus your

concerns, sharpen your questions, and develop answers that are your own. Give it a try!

SHARE WITH OTHERS

Everyone needs a friend with whom to share thoughts and doubts. How rich we are if we have such a friend. We know that no matter how rotten we feel or how unloving we sound, that person loves us and accepts us!

One approach is to gather a small group of people who may be ready to explore the meaning of life and death together, and to be supportive of one another as you do so. Commit yourselves to a specific number of meetings on a regular—weekly—basis for a specified period.

You may wish to study a certain book as a basis for your sharing. A good volume for this purpose is *Life, Death, and Destiny* by Roger L. Shinn.

A less structured approach would be to invite a group to view a thought-provoking play, movie, or TV program together and then discuss it over coffee. Or you might want to loan a good book to a friend and then share your ideas after you've both read it.

A study book or a movie can provide a common starting point—a good beginning. But hopefully you will soon feel free enough to move into the realm of personal ideas and questions. It is amazing to me how many people carry around a burden of guilt about questions they were afraid to ask. They simply assume that "a Christian shouldn't have doubts about that!" Actually, no question, if seriously asked, is unchristian!

Let me repeat. No question is unchristian! We, like the father of the possessed child, need continually to pray, "I believe; help my unbelief!" (Mark 9:24). But how can we honestly pray this prayer if we deny our unbelief ?

The Christian gospel is truth. And truth can withstand any searching question we might ask. When we dare to ask the questions that haunt us, we often find others with the same unasked questions. We find a new freedom, then, to search for answers together.

Increasingly, persons with similar interests and concerns—single parents, alcoholics, gamblers, parents whose babies died of crib death—are experiencing the help that can be found through sharing. A book that has some concrete suggestions for successful small groups is *New Life in the Church* by Robert Raines.

EXPERIENCES THAT CAN HELP

A sharing group or an individual can find plenty of opportunities today for experiencing closer contact with death. Although experience may not always be the best teacher, it does teach. But to find the experience it may be necessary to go to the nursing homes and hospitals in which our society has hidden away our dying members. We need to make a conscious effort to be with these persons.

Hospitals and nursing homes are always looking for volunteers to visit with and read to the patients, to write letters for them, and just to be there regularly so the lonely will have persons to relate to and visits to look forward to. Volunteer work provides an excellent opportunity to gain real insight into life and death as well as to meet people at the point of their need and grow to love them.

Children's wards in large hospitals are also in need of volunteers. It's a real challenge, often shocking and even painful, to care for these little ones and then lose them. But many people find that a child's smile can open up new perspectives on life and death that make the pain worth experiencing.

Experiences like these help us to appreciate the account of the distraught mother whose only son died when a poisonous snake bit him. She confronted Buddha, pleading that he bring her son back to life. Buddha, so the story goes, told her that first she must bring him mustard seeds from five families who knew no grief. The mother rushed out, filled with hope. Years later she returned empty handed. Buddha, in his wisdom asked, "Did you really think that you were alone in your grief ?" We too can find strength to face our own grief by sharing the grief and pain of others.

No matter how often we have faced the meaning of

life and death, even in such volunteer work, the first time we walk into a casket display room is likely to be an overpowering experience. It certainly was for me. Even if the morbidity is not overwhelming, the choices that confront us are staggering.

Usually, morticians are glad to make arrangements for classes, small groups, or individuals to come and visit the funeral home and talk with them about funeral practices. They will answer your questions and give you a tour of their facilities. I have found this to be extremely helpful. It gives us time to work through our beliefs and to sort out our values at a time when we are not under the stress and pressures imposed by the death of a loved one.

It is also worthwhile to take the time to plan your own funeral. The very idea may seem morbid to you. But think with me, if you will, of some of the benefits. The exercise can be a valuable tool for working through your own beliefs about dying and your own feelings about modern funeral practices. A high school teacher who has her classes do this told me that more than one student has changed life styles after struggling to write his own obituary! Planning our own funeral can force us to face the meaning of our life as well as of our death.

While the funeral plans we devise aren't binding after our death, they can take a tremendous weight off of our survivors. The bereaved won't have to guess—and perhaps disagree—about what we would have wanted. They won't have to feel guilty over the price of the casket if we have already made our wishes known. The minister and mortician will also appreciate any guidelines we may have left concerning the service and burial. All in all, the benefits for those who choose this approach are many.

Once we have made our plans, what do we do with them? There are a variety of options. Some may include them in their log as a way of thinking through their own beliefs, not intending for them actually to be used or even for anyone else to see them. A notation to this effect might be helpful to your survivors. Others may want to give copies to their family or their pastor or both. Some people file a copy with a funeral director at the funeral home. There is little value in putting a copy with your will, since the will is usually not opened until after the funeral.

Making a will can be one of the most basic and important ways to face the fact of our own death. Yet many people never "get around to it." The number who "put off " doing it is staggering. At least by the time they become parents a couple should make their wills. Ideally, every adult should have one.

Parents should also make concrete arrangements for the care of their children in the event both parents are killed. Talking about it is the first step. Once a decision has been made, the person or persons you have chosen should be asked if they would be willing to assume the added responsibility. Then your children and your families should be told. Hopefully, this would avoid the added tragedy of battles over custody in the event of the death of both parents.

Taking the time to share with your children the plans you have made for them can be really rewarding. It provides a good chance for helping the family grow together in their understanding of life and death.

Earlier I mentioned that our children know they will live with their godparents if my husband and I both die. We have had a number of interesting conversations about this as various situations have arisen.

Once when it looked like I would be facing major surgery for the second time in two years, I commented at the breakfast table, "You know, kids, if I die, I'd want daddy to get married again."

"You would?!" came the incredulous reply of seven-year-old Peter. After thinking for a moment, he continued, "Well, then, don't you worry about that, mom. I'll take care of it!"

His response made us smile. But I have seen children plagued by guilt whenever they expressed affection to a stepparent because they felt they were being disloyal to their dead or divorced parent. Talking about life and death situations can be of tremendous value for facing them when they come.

Check the laws in your state. In many states the courts have the responsibility of awarding custody of children in the event of the parents' death. It may not be possible to put your choice for guardians in your will, but it is proper to include a letter of intent with your will which informs the court of your wishes and requests that the court act accordingly. It is a good idea to update this from time to time as situations change. Even if you don't change the will or the letter of intent, a fairly current date might be valuable. It is only in rare situations that the court would not follow the parents' request.

Sometimes we forego the opportunity to visit dying friends and to attend funerals. How many times we've said with regret, "I really meant to. . . ." When we are truly able to face and accept death, we will more likely give this matter higher priority. But sometimes acceptance comes as the result of just such visitation and attendance.

Remembering our bereaved friends and relatives a week or a month after the funeral is another often-neglected opportunity. We gain much ourselves when we are comfortable enough about death to be there with the bereaved, to leave the door open for conversation about the dead person and about grief.

When we are able to face death ourselves and to meet others at their point of need, we are already well on our way to helping children face death. We will begin to find that death comes up naturally in conversations—this is as it should be. We will convey positive attitudes about death by the way we live. What more could we want?

In a famous prayer that has come down to us from the thirteenth century, St. Francis of Assisi summarizes the affirmations of faith with respect to death even as he mentions the kinds of life experiences that contribute to its building:

> Lord, make me an instrument of Thy peace;
> Where there is hatred, let me sow love;
> Where there is injury, pardon;
> Where there is doubt, faith;
> Where there is despair, hope;
> Where there is darkness, light;
> Where there is sadness, joy.
>
> O Divine Master,
>   Grant that I may not so much seek to be consoled as to console!
>   To be understood as to understand;
>   To be loved as to love.
> For it is in giving that we receive,
> It is in pardoning that we are pardoned,
> And it is in dying that we are born to eternal life.

May it be so for you and for me!

EIGHT

Putting It All Together

DEATH is a part of LIFE.
It is real,
permanent,
and universal.

Facing death means
facing our fears
and doubts
and anger
and guilt
as we struggle to find meaning in life—
and death.

ACCEPTANCE comes as a gift from God.
As we share in the grace of his forgiving love
we come to understand that the power of love
overcomes the fear of death
and we receive the gift of eternal life
through Jesus Christ.

To help children grow in their understanding of death—
we must LISTEN,
beginning where the child is;
we must ACCEPT

their fears and guilt and anger and questions
    as part of the reality they must face;
we must MEET INDIVIDUAL NEEDS,
    loving, caring, being there;
we must BE HONEST,
    giving simple answers to questions children
    ask—
        while neither denying death
        nor blaming God;
we must SHARE *OUR* FAITH,
    first by our living
        and then in honest responses to needs ex-
        pressed by the child,
            always being careful to do so
                in ways that leave the door open for the
                child
                    to find faith that is his or her own!

May our living and our dying lead our children to
understand and affirm that

    "Death is swallowed up in victory.
      O death, where is thy victory?
      O death, where is thy sting?"

      The sting of death is sin
        And the power of sin is the law.
    But thanks be to God
      who gives us the victory
        through our Lord Jesus Christ.
                        (1 Cor. 15:54–57)

Let it be so! Amen!

Notes

1. Leo Tolstoy, *The Death of Ivan Ilych and Other Stories* (New York: Signet Classic, 1960), p. 137. Used by permission of Oxford University Press.

2. Ibid., p. 153.

3. Janet Chusmir, *The DesMoines Register*, 24 September 1973, p. 13 (copyright Knight News Wire).

4. Earl A. Grollman, *Talking about Death: A Dialogue Between Parent and Child* (Boston: Beacon Press, 1970), p. 18. This is the best book I know of for Christian and Jewish parents to use with their children as they talk about the meaning of death.

5. Reuel Howe, *Man's Need and God's Action* (Greenwich, Conn.: Seabury Press, 1953), p. 153. Used by permission.

6. Walter M. Miller, Jr., *A Canticle for Leibowitz* (New York: Bantam Books, 1959), p. 242. Copyright © 1959, by Walter Miller, Jr. Reprinted by permission of Harold Matson Company, Inc.

7. John A. T. Robinson, "The Body: A Study in Pauline Theology," *Studies in Biblical Theology*, no. 5 (London: SCM, 1952), p. 14.

8. Edwin Shneidman, "You and Death," *Psychology Today* 5, no. 1 (June 1971):76. Copyright © 1971 Ziff-Davis Publishing Company.

9. Michel Quoist, *Prayers* (New York: Sheed and Ward, 1963), pp. 41–43.

Additional Resources

ABOUT CHILDREN

Agee, James. *Death in the Family*. New York: Bantam Books, 1971.

Fargues, Marie. *The Child and the Mystery of Death*. Glen Rock, N. J.: Paulist Press, 1966.

Grollman, Earl A., ed. *Explaining Death to Children*. Boston: Beacon Press, 1967.

Jackson, Edgar N. *Telling a Child about Death*. New York: Channel Press, 1965.

Nagy, Maria H. "The Child's View of Death," *The Meaning of Death*. Edited by Herman Feifel. New York: McGraw-Hill, 1959. Pp. 79–98.

Reed, Elizabeth Liggett. *Helping Children with the Mystery of Death*. Nashville: Abingdon, 1970.

FOR CHILDREN

Grollman, Earl A. *Talking about Death*. Boston: Beacon Press, 1970.

Harris, Audrey. *Why Did He Die?* Minneapolis: Lerner Publications Co., 1965.

Lewis, C. S. *The Chronicles of Narnia* (includes: *The Lion, the Witch, and the Wardrobe; Prince Caspian; The Voyage of the Dawn Treader; The Silver Chair; The Horse and His Boy; The Magician's Nephew; The Last Battle*). New York: Collier Books, 1970.

White, E. B. *Charlotte's Web*. New York: Harper & Row, 1952.

84

GENERAL RESOURCES

Feifel, Herman, ed. *The Meaning of Death.* New York: McGraw-Hill, 1959.

Jackson, Edgar. *The Christian Funeral: Its Meaning, Its Purpose, and Its Modern Practice.* New York: Channel Press, 1966.

_____. *When Someone Dies.* Philadelphia: Fortress Press, 1971.

Kubler-Ross, Elizabeth. *On Death and Dying.* New York: Macmillan Co., 1969.

Matthews, Joseph W. "The Time My Father Died," *The Modern Vision of Death.* Edited by Nathan A. Scott, Jr. Richmond, Va.: John Knox Press, 1967.

Scott, Nathan A., Jr., ed. *The Modern Vision of Death.* Richmond, Va.: John Knox Press, 1967.

Shinn, Roger L. *Life, Death and Destiny.* Philadelphia: Westminster Press, 1957.

Shneidman, Edwin S. "Death Questionnaire," *Psychology Today* 4, no. 3 (August 1970):67–72.

_____. "You and Death," *Psychology Today* 5, no. 1 (June 1971):43ff.

Switzer, David K. *The Dynamics of Grief.* Nashville: Abingdon, 1970.

Westberg, Granger E. *Good Grief.* Philadelphia: Fortress Press, 1962.

LITERATURE

Dooley, Thomas A. *Doctor Tom Dooley, My Story.* New York: Farrar, Straus & Co., Ariel Books, 1960.

Frank, Anne. *The Diary of a Young Girl.* New York: Doubleday & Co., 1952.

Gunther, John. *Death Be Not Proud.* New York: Harper & Bro., 1949.

Miller, Arthur. *Death of a Salesman.* New York: Viking Press, 1949.

Miller, Walter M., Jr. *A Canticle for Leibewitz.* New York: Bantam Books, 1959.

Saint-Exupery, Antoine de. *The Little Prince.* New York: Harcourt, Brace & Co., 1943.

Tolstoy, Leo. *The Death of Ivan Ilych and Other Stories.* New York: Signet Classics, 1960. Pp. 95–156.

THEOLOGY AND DEATH

Cargas, Harry J., and White, Ann, S. L., eds. *Death and Hope.* New York: Corpus Books, 1970.

Cullmann, Oscar. *Christ and Time.* Philadelphia: Westminster Press, 1950.

Guardini, Romano. *The Last Things.* Notre Dame, Ind.: University of Notre Dame Press, 1954.

Rahner, Karl. *On the Theology of Death.* New York: Herder & Herder, 1961.

Thielicke, Helmut. *Death and Life.* Philadelphia: Fortress Press, 1970.

Tillich, Paul. "The Eternal Now," *The Modern Vision of Death.* Edited by Nathan A. Scott, Jr. Richmond, Va.: John Knox Press, 1967. Pp. 97–106.